NOW YOU CAN READ....
THE CREATION

STORY RETOLD BY LEONARD MATTHEWS

ILLUSTRATED BY LYNNE WILLEY

Published by Rourke Publications, Inc., P.O. Box 3328, Vero
Beach, Florida 32964. Copyright © 1984 by Rourke Publica-
tions, Inc. All copyrights reserved. No part of this book may
be reproduced in any form without written permission from
the publisher. Printed in the United States of America.
   The Publishers acknowledge permission from Brimax
Books for the use of the name "Now You Can Read" and
"Large Type For First Readers" which identify Brimax Now
You Can Read series.

Library of Congress Cataloging in Publication Data

Matthews, Leonard.
  The creation.

  (Now you can read Bible stories)
  Summary: Retells the Bible story of the Creation
and the Garden of Eden.
  1. Creation—Biblical teaching—Juvenile literature.
2. Bible stories, English—O.T.   Genesis.   [1. Creation.
2. Adam (Biblical character)   3. Eve (Biblical character)
4. Bible stories—O.T.]   I. Title.   II. Series:
Now you can read—Bible stories.
BS651.M39   1984   233'.11   84-15125
ISBN 0-86625-305-X

GROLIER ENTERPRISES CORP.

NOW YOU CAN READ.....

THE CREATION

Once, there was no world. There was only darkness. It was God who made our world. He took six days to do this. First, there had to be light. So, on the first day He made light. On the second day, He created the sky above us. On the third day, God gathered all the seas together in one place. Then, He made the dry land. Over the land He dropped seeds.

Flowers and trees grew from the seeds. During the fourth day He placed the sun, the moon and the stars in the sky. On the fifth day, God brought living creatures to our world.

He put the fish into the sea.
He made all the birds. The sixth
day was the most special of all.
That was when He made all the
land animals and the first man.
The man was called Adam. God
wanted Adam to be happy. He
gave him a beautiful garden.
It was named the Garden of
Eden. The word Eden means
"delight." It was the right
word for this lovely garden.

Beautiful trees and sweet
smelling flowers were everywhere.
There were two special trees. One
was the Tree of Life. Adam could
eat its fruit and live forever.
The other was the Tree of Knowledge
of Good and Evil. On the Seventh
day, God rested. He had finished
making the world.

Adam was a very happy man. The rivers were full of fish. All sorts of animals roamed everywhere. There was much fruit to eat. It seemed as though he needed nothing.

Adam was the first man in a new world. There was so much for him to do. For a long time he enjoyed himself. Then, he began to feel lonely. Adam was the only human in the Garden of Eden.

There were many kinds of animals. There was only one human. Adam wanted someone like himself to whom he could talk.

God was watching Adam. He saw that Adam was unhappy because he was so lonely.

God felt sorry for Adam. One night He came and made Adam fall into a very deep sleep. While he slept, God took a rib from his side. He did not hurt Adam. From the rib God made a woman. She was called Eve.

"Live happily together," said God, "but remember this. You must not eat the fruit of the Tree of Knowledge of Good and Evil. If you do, your happy days will be over forever. Never forget what I am telling you." Adam and Eve knew that they must obey God. There was no reason why they should not have lived happily ever after.

For a long time all was well. Adam was no longer lonely. Eve was a good wife. Then, one day, their happy life came to an end. Eve was resting near the Tree of Knowledge of Good and Evil. It stood in the center of the Garden of Eden. Suddenly, Eve was surprised to see a large snake.

The snake was crawling toward her. When it saw Eve it stopped and said, "I hear that God has told you that you must never eat the fruit of that tree." Eve nodded. "Yes," she replied. "God has told us that if we do our happy life will be over."

The snake laughed. "How could that be?" it asked. "If you eat the fruit you will be like God."

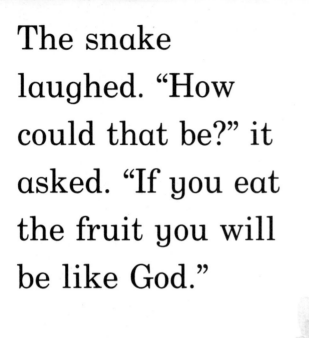

Eve's eyes opened wide. "How could that be?" she asked the snake.

"Because," replied the evil snake, "after you have eaten the fruit, you will understand what is good and what is evil."

"Good? Evil?" wondered Eve. She did not understand. In the Garden of Eden there had only been happiness. What was good? What was evil?

"Eat the fruit," the snake whispered. "Then you *will* understand." Eve forgot God's warning. She ate some of the fruit.

Then the snake crawled away. It had finished its evil work.
Eve was now even more foolish. She gave some of the forbidden fruit to Adam. Now they both had new thoughts. They knew not only what it was to be good. They knew what it was to be evil.

They had disobeyed God. They
knew that He would punish
them.
They ran away and hid as best
they could.

It was impossible to hide from God. He knew where to find them. He called to them, "Why are you hiding?"

Adam had to tell God the truth. "So, you have both broken faith with me," God said. "You must be punished."

God gave them some skins to wear as clothes. He sent them out of the Garden of Eden, never to return. Because they had not obeyed God their happy days were over forever. How foolish they had been.

All these appear in the pages of the story. Can you find them?

fruit

Adam

Eve

snake

Tree of Life   Tree of Knowledge
of Good and Evil.

frog

Garden of Eden

Now tell the story in your own words.